© 2002 by Barbour Publishing, Inc.

ISBN 1-58660-442-2

Cover art © Photodisc, Inc.

Published by Barbour Books, an imprint of Barbour Publishing, Inc., P.O. Box 719, Uhrichsville, Ohio 44683
www.barbourbooks.com

Member of the
Evangelical Christian
Publishers Association

Printed in China.

For A Special Grandmother

KELLY KOHL

DayMaker
GREETING BOOKS

CONTENTS

A Grandmother Is Love. . .

Love is the beauty of the soul.

ST. AUGUSTINE

What Are Grandmas For?

Grandmas are for stories about things of long ago.
Grandmas are for caring about all the things you know.
Grandmas are for rocking you and singing you to sleep.
Grandmas are for giving you nice memories to keep.
Grandmas are for knowing
all the things you're dreaming of.
But, most of all, grandmas are for love.

AUTHOR UNKNOWN

From the time I was a child, I never once doubted my grandmother's love. She was always there for me with words of encouragement, a warm smile, and lots of hugs. She was ready to forgive me if I made a mistake. She never judged me, just loved me.

Grandma was like that with all of her grandchildren. We were all treated fairly. One of us never received a more expensive gift at Christmastime than the others. And if the difference in price was only a dollar, Grandma made sure we received that dollar in an envelope with our gift. We all felt special. . .because she emphasized how special we were to her—and to Jesus.

As I've grown, I now see how her love for her grandchildren was a perfect model of Christ's love for His children.

Perfect love sometimes does not come
until grandchildren are born.

WELSH PROVERB

*We grow old as soon as
we cease to love and trust.*

MADAME DE CHOISEUL

Life is a journey,
and love is what makes that journey worthwhile.

AUTHOR UNKNOWN

Love is patient, love is kind.
It does not envy, it does not boast, it is not proud.
It is not rude, it is not self-seeking, it is not easily angered,
it keeps no record of wrongs.
Love does not delight in evil but rejoices with the truth.
It always protects, always trusts,
always hopes, always perseveres.
Love never fails.

1 CORINTHIANS 13:4–8

*We are shaped and fashioned
by what we love.*

JOHANN WOLFGANG VON GOETHE

9

*Grandmothers and grandchildren
have a lot in common.*

PAM BROWN

It is only with the heart that one can see rightly;
what is essential is invisible to the eye.

ANTOINE DE SAINT-EXUPERY

A mother becomes a true
grandmother the day she stops
noticing the terrible things her
children do because she is so
enchanted with the wonderful
things her grandchildren do.

LOIS WYSE

Love comforteth like sunshine after rain.

WILLIAM SHAKESPEARE

The supreme happiness of life is
the conviction that we are loved;
loved for ourselves, or rather, loved
in spite of ourselves.

VICTOR HUGO

Surely, two of the most satisfying experiences in life must be those of being a grandchild or a grandparent.

DONALD A. NORBERG

Love must be sincere. . . .
Honor one another above yourselves.

ROMANS 12:9–10

If becoming a grandmother
was only a matter of choice,
I should advise every one of you
straight away to become one.

HANNAH WHITALL SMITH

Nobody can do for little children
what grandparents do.
Grandparents sort of sprinkle stardust
over the lives of little children.

ALEX HALEY

Grandmother-grandchild relationships are simple.
Grandmas are short on criticism and long on love.

GRANDMA JAN

To love abundantly
is to live abundantly.

AUTHOR UNKNOWN

Above all, love each other deeply,
because love covers over a multitude of sins.

1 PETER 4:8

The love we give away
is the only love we keep.

ELBERT HUBBARD

We should love one another.

1 JOHN 3:11

A Grandmother Is Wisdom. . .

True wisdom lies in gathering the
precious things out of each day as it goes by.

E. S. BOUTON

Grandparents

Grandparents bestow upon their grandchildren
The strength and wisdom that time
And experience have given them.
Grandchildren bless their grandparents
With a youthful vitality and innocence
That help them stay young at heart forever.
Together they create a chain of love
Linking the past with the future.
The chain may lengthen,
But it will never part.

AUTHOR UNKNOWN

She never spoke the words harshly, though she made sure her opinion was known. No matter what advice she offered me, I always came around to the conclusion that Grandma was right.

I would spend countless weekends at her house, sharing my hopes and dreams with her over hours of Scrabble. (I could never beat Grandma at that game—not ever!) In return, she gave me advice for living—advice that I would look back on with thanks. She taught me to honor God. . .and to look to Him for guidance in my life.

Never have I met a woman who loved God more than she did. If I could ever strive to be like anyone on this earth, it would be my grandmother. She was a beacon of light in our family—an amazing woman whose faith in God was stronger than anything else in her life.

Knowledge comes, but wisdom lingers.

CALVIN COOLIDGE

But godliness with contentment is great gain.

1 TIMOTHY 6:6

A child's life is like a piece of paper on which every person leaves a mark.

CHINESE PROVERB

19

You Know You're a Grandparent When You Offer Words of Wisdom Like:

- Life does not cease to be funny when people die any more than it ceases to be serious when people laugh.

  GEORGE BERNARD SHAW

- It is good to have an end to journey toward; but it is the journey that matters, in the end.

  URSULA K. LEGUIN

- Health: To eat what you don't want, drink what you don't like, and do what you'd rather not.

  MARK TWAIN

- Unless someone like you cares a whole awful lot, nothing is going to get better. It's not.

  DR. SEUSS

Wisdom is the power to put our time
and our knowledge to the proper use.

THOMAS J. WATSON

*If you would civilize a man,
begin with his grandmother.*

VICTOR HUGO

Wisdom is not wisdom when it is
derived from books alone.

HORACE

The secret things belong to the LORD our God,
but the things revealed belong to us
and to our children forever,
that we may follow all the words of this law.

DEUTERONOMY 29:29

I will pour out my Spirit on your offspring,
and my blessing on your descendants.

ISAIAH 44:3

A Grandmother Is Beautiful Memories. . .

Memories are all we really own.

Elias Lieberman

For a Special Grandmother

When Time who steals our years away
Shall steal our pleasures too,
The mem'ry of the past will stay,
And half our joys renew.

THOMAS MOORE

Memories last forever, never do they die.

MELINA CAMPOS

You are told a lot about your education,
but some beautiful, sacred memory,
preserved since childhood,
is perhaps the best education of all.

FYODOR DOSTOEVSKI

After I spent the weekend at her house, Grandma used to drive me to church every Sunday. On the way, she'd help me learn my Bible verse for Sunday school, and we'd sing some of my favorite songs.

It amazes me now that something which was seemingly so insignificant—just a part of everyday life—could have impacted my life so much. During those car rides, I learned how important Jesus is, and I learned to have a strong faith in Him. Because of Grandma's example, my faith remains steady even today.

Whenever I think back on these memories, my heart smiles. . . . I thank God for giving me such a sweet grandmother who influenced my life in such a profound way.

We spend our years as a tale that is told.

PSALM 90:9 KJV

What we learn with pleasure we never forget.

ALFRED MERCIER

And life is what we make it—
always has been, always will be.

GRANDMA MOSES

If I could reach up and hold a star for every time you've made me smile, the entire evening sky would be in the palm of my hand.

AUTHOR UNKNOWN

You will find as you look back upon your life, that the moments when you have really lived are the moments when you have done things in the spirit of love.

HENRY DRUMMOND

The heart has its own memory like the mind,
And in it are enshrined the precious keepsakes,
into which is wrought
The givers' loving thought.

HENRY WADSWORTH LONGFELLOW

*God gave us memory
so we might have roses in December.*

ITALO SVEVO

To show a child what has once delighted you,
to find the child's delight added to your own,
so that there is now a double delight seen
in the glow of trust and affection, this is happiness.

J. B. PRIESTLEY

. . .tomorrow they will be

somebody's good old days.

GERALD BARZAN

Life isn't a matter of milestones but of moments.

ROSE FITZGERALD KENNEDY

A Grandmother Is a True Friend...

A friend is one who walks in when others walk out.

WALTER WINCHELL

If instead of a gem, or even a flower,
we could cast the gift of a lovely thought
into the heart of a friend,
that would be giving as the angels give.

GEORGE MACDONALD

A friend may well be reckoned

the masterpiece of nature.

RALPH WALDO EMERSON

Thou wert my guide, philosopher, and friend.

ALEXANDER POPE

Who better to sit down with and enjoy a hot fudge sundae and a lot of giggles? Grandmas are true friends for life. Nowhere else can you find such a friend.

- Grandmas never hold a grudge.

- Grandmas love to listen to your stories.

- Grandmas share your hopes and dreams.

  In all the world, no one can take the place of a grandma!

Ah, how good it feels. . .
the hand of an old friend.

MARY ENGLEBRIGHT

But it is you. . .my close friend.

PSALM 55:13

No soul is so desolate as long as there is
a human being for whom
it can feel trust and reverence.

GEORGE ELIOT

To our grandchildren,
we are the owners of heirlooms
and the source of their history. . .
soft pillows, home-baked cookies,
and the hoarse voice after ball games. . . .
We are the playmates who offer security,
help with chores, give second opinions (unbiased),
and can read nine books aloud at a sitting.

C. ELLEN WATTS,
Over 60 and Picking Up Speed

A friend is one who knows us

but loves us anyway.

FR. JEROME CUMMINGS

Our mouths were filled with laughter,
our tongues with songs of joy.

PSALM 126:2

Friendship is the source of the greatest pleasures.

ST. THOMAS AQUINAS

It is not so much our friends' help that helps us
as the confident knowledge that they will help us.

EPICURUS

Friendship needs no words.

DAG HAMMARSKJOLD

The friendship that can cease has never been real.

SAINT JEROME

A friend loves at all times.

PROVERBS 17:17

Friendship that flows from the heart
cannot be frozen by adversity,
as the water that flows from the spring
cannot congeal in winter.

JAMES FENIMORE COOPER

A friend, as it were, is a second self.

MARCUS T. CICERO

Never shall I forget the days I spent with you.
Continue to be my friend,
as you will always find me yours.

LUDWIG VAN BEETHOVEN

I have called you friends. . . .

JOHN 15:15 KJV